The Secret Sins of Economics

The Secret Sins of Economics

Deirdre McCloskey

PRICKLY PARADIGM PRESS
CHICAGO

Prickly Paradigm Press, LLC
5629 South University Avenue
Chicago, Il 60637

www.prickly-paradigm.com

ISBN: 0-9717575-3-4
LCCN: 2002 102650

Printed in the United States of America on acid-free
paper.

What's sinful about economics is not what the average anthropologist or historian or journalist thinks. From the outside the dismal science seems *obviously* sinful, if irritatingly influential. But the obvious sins are not all that terrible; or, if terrible, they are committed anyway by everybody else. It is actually two particular, non-obvious, and unusual sins, two secret ones, that cripple the scientific enterprise—in economics and in a few other fields nowadays (like psychology and political science and medical science and population biology).

Yet a sympathetic critic who says these things and wishes that her own beloved economics would grow up and start focusing all its energies on doing proper science (the way physics or geology or anthropology or history or certain parts of literary criticism do it) finds

2

herself sadly misunderstood. The commonplace and
venial sins block scrutiny of the bizarre and mortal
ones. Pity the poor sympathetic critic, construed regu-
larly to be making this or that Idiot's Critique: "Oh, I
see. You're one of those airy humanists who just can't
stand to think of numbers or mathematics." Or, "Oh, I
see. When you say economics is 'rhetorical' you want
economists to write more warmly."

I tell you it's maddening. The sympathetic critic,
herself an economist, even a Chicago-School economist, slowly during twenty years of groping came to
recognize the ubiquity of the Two Secret Sins of
Economics (in the end they are one, deriving from
pride, as all sins do). She has developed helpful sugges-
tions for redeeming economics from sin. And yet no
one—not the anthropologist or English professor or
others from the outside certainly, but least of all the
economist or medical scientist—grasps her point, or
acts on it.

VIRTUES MISIDENTIFIED AS SINS

Quantification

Quantification, though, is not a sin. Numbers came
with social science at its birth. The English political
arithmeticians William Petty and Gregory King and
the rest in the late seventeenth century (anticipated in
the early seventeenth century by, like so much of what

we call English, certain Dutchmen) wanted most to
know How Much. It was an entirely novel obsession.
You might call it bourgeois. How Much will it cost to
drain the Somerset Levels? How Much does England's
treasure by foreign trade depend on possessing
colonies? How Much is this and How Much that?
The blessed Adam Smith a century later kept
wondering How Much wages in Edinburgh differed
from those in London (too much), and How Much the
colonies by then acquired in England's incessant eighteenth-century wars against France were worth to the
home country (not much). By the late eighteenth
century, it is surprising to note, the statistical chart had
been invented; what isn't surprising is that it hadn't
been invented before—another sign that quantitative
thinking was novel, at least in the West (the Chinese
had been collecting statistics on population and prices
for centuries). European states from Sweden to Naples
began in the eighteenth century collecting statistics to
worry about: prices, population, balances of trade, flows
of gold. The word "statistics" was a coinage of
German and Italian enthusiasts for state action in the
early eighteenth century, pointing to a story of the state
use of numbering. Then dawned the age of statistics,
and everything from drug incarcerations and smoking
deaths to the value of a life and the credit rating of Jane
Q. Public are numbered.

It became a sort of insanity, of course. Tour guides
observe that American men want to know how tall
every tower is, how many bricks there are in every
notable wall, how many died here, how many lived.

Samuel Johnson was in 1775 typical of his age and his gender in reporting the size of everything he encountered in his tour of the West of Scotland (he used his walking stick as a measuring rod). By the 1850s the conservative critics of capitalism, such as Charles Dickens, were becoming very cross about statistics:

> Thomas Gradgrind, sir—peremptorily Thomas—Thomas Gradgrind. With a rule and a pair of scales, and the multiplication table always in his pocket, sir, ready to weigh and measure any parcel of human nature, and tell you exactly what it comes to. It is a mere question of figures, a case of simple arithmetic...
>
> "Father," she still pursued, "does Mr Bounderby ask me to love him?"
>
> "...[T]he reply depends so materially, Louisa, on the sense in which we use the expression. Now, Mr Bounderby does not do you the injustice, and does not do himself the injustice, of pretending to anything fanciful, fantastic, or (I am using synonymous terms) sentimental....Therefore, perhaps the expression itself—I merely suggest this to you, my dear—may be a little misplaced."
>
> "What would you advise me to use in its stead, father?"
>
> "Why, my dear Louisa," said Mr. Gradgrind, completely recovered by this time, "I would advise you (since you ask me) to consider this question, as you have been accustomed to consider every other question, simply as one of tangible Fact. The ignorant and the giddy may embarrass such subjects with irrelevant fancies, and other absurdities that have no existence, properly viewed—really no existence—but

it is no compliment to you to say, that you know better. Now, what are the Facts of this case? You are, we will say in round numbers, twenty years of age; Mr. Bounderby is, we will say in round numbers, fifty....[T]he question arises, Is this one disparity sufficient to operate as a bar to such a marriage? In considering this question, it is not unimportant to take into account the statistics of marriage, so far as they have yet been obtained, in England and Wales. I find, on reference to the figures, that a large proportion of these marriages are contracted between parties of very unequal ages, and that the elder of these contracting parties is, in rather more than three-fourths of these instances, the bridegroom. It is remarkable as showing the wide prevalence of this law, that among the natives of the British possessions in India, also in a consid-erable part of China, and among the Calmucks of Tartary, the best means of computation yet furnished us by travelers, yield similar results."

Counting can surely be a nitwit's, or the Devil's, tool. Among the more unnerving exhibits in the extermina-tion camp at Auschwitz are the books in which Hitler's willing executioners kept records on every person they killed.

The formal and mathematical theory of statistics was largely invented in the 1880s by eugenicists (those clever racists at the origin of so much in the social sciences) and perfected in the twentieth century by agronomists (yes, agronomists, at places like the Rothamsted agricultural experiment station in England or at Iowa State University). The newly mathematized statistics became a fetish in wannabe sciences. During the 1920s, when sociology was a young science, quantification was a way of claiming status, as it became also in economics, fresh from putting aside its old name of political economy, and in psychology, fresh from a separation from philosophy. In the 1920s and 1930s even the social anthropologists, those men and women of the fanciful, fantastic, or (I am using synonymous terms) sentimental, counted coconuts.

And the economists, oh, the economists, how they counted, and still count. Take any copy of *The American Economic Review* to hand (surely you subscribe?) and open it at random. To perhaps Joel Waldfogel, "The Deadweight Loss of Christmas" (no kidding: December 1993; Waldfogel is arguing that since a gift is not chosen by the recipient it is not worth what the giver spent, which leads to a loss compared with merely sending cash. Who could not love such a science of Prudence?). On p. 1331 you will find the following Table 1:

Average Amounts Paid
and Values of Gifts

Variable	Survey 1	Survey 2
Amount paid ($)	438.2	508.9
Value ($)	313.4	462.1
Percentage ratio of average value to average paid	71.5	90.8
Number of recipients	86	58

It is a mere question of figures, a case of simple arithmetic.

Refutatio: But after all, think about it. When you *want* to count your coconuts, or the cash value of your Christmas gifts, it makes sense to do the job right. Many of the things we wish to know come in quantitative form. It matters—not absolutely, in God's eyes, but for particular human purposes—how much it will rain tomorrow and how much it rained yesterday. For sound practical and spiritual reasons we wish sometimes to know How Much. How many slaves were driven from Africa? Perhaps 29 million (the population of Britain at the height of the slave trade was about 8 million), more than half going east, not west, across the Sahara or the Indian Ocean, not the Atlantic. How has Cuba fared under Communism and the American embargo? Income per head in Cuba has fallen by a third since 1959, while in the Dominican Republic, Chile, Mexico, Brazil, and indeed in Latin America and the Caribbean generally it has more than doubled. How big is immigration to the United States now? Smaller in proportion to population than it was in 1910. And on and on and on.

(You can see from the examples that no claim is being made here that numbers are by nature peculiarly "objective," whatever that pop-philosophical term might exactly mean, or "non-political," or "scientific." Numbers are rhetoric, which is to say humanly persuasive. We agree in a persuasive culture to assign meaning to this or that number, and then can be persuaded to this or that view of the matter. Pebbles lie around, as Richard Rorty has put it; facts of the matter do not. It is our human decision to count or weigh or mix the pebbles in constituting the pebbly facts.)

Economists are selected for their great love of numbers. The joke is, "I'm an economist because I didn't have enough personality to become an accountant." A statistical argument is always honored in the Department of Economics. Many non-economists on the contrary fear numbers, dislike them, dishonor them, are confused and irritated by them. But some important questions can only be answered numerically. A great many other questions are at least helpfully illuminated by numbers. Your age number is not the only important fact about you, and is certainly nothing like your full Meaning ("You are, we will say in round numbers, twenty years of age; Mr Bounderby is, we will say in round numbers, fifty"). But it is a number helpful for some purposes— ordinary conversation, for one thing; medical examination for another; yes, even marriage. It's humanly useful to know that you grew up in the 1950s and came of age in the liberating 1960s: age sixty on September 11, 2002 (happy birthday). Temperature is not the only measure of a good day. Wind, sunshine, human events, and human-assigned significance matter. That this is the month and this the happy morn of Christ's nativity has meaning beyond 30°F. But it is worth knowing that the temperature on the blessed day was not -459.67°F or 212°F.

So counting is not a sin of economics. It is a virtue.

Mathematics

Nor is mathematics a sin. Mathematics is not identical
to counting or statistics. The newspapers chortle
when they find a mathematician who cannot balance
his checkbook, but that's just a misunderstanding of
what mathematicians do. There have been some
famously good calculators among mathematicians, the
eighteenth-century Swiss mathematician Leonhard
Euler being an instance (he also knew the entire *Aeneid*
by heart; in Latin, I need hardly add). But odd as it
sounds, most of mathematics has nothing to do with
actual *numbers*. Euler used calculation in the same way
that mathematicians nowadays use computers, for
back-of-the-envelope tests of hunches on the way to
developing what the mathematicians are pleased to call
a *real* proof of such amazing facts as: $e^{\pi i} + 1 = 0$ (and
therefore God exists). You can have a "real" proof, the
style of demonstration developed by the Greeks (with
which you became acquainted in high-school geom-
etry, either loving or hating it), without examining a
single number or even a single concrete example.
Thus: the Pythagorean Theorem is true for *any* right
triangle, regardless of its dimensions, and is proven not
by induction from many or even zillions of numerical
examples of right triangles, but universally and for all
time, praise God, may her name be glorified, by
deduction from premises. Accept the premises and
you have accepted the Theorem. *Quod erat demon-
strandum.*

Statistics or other quantitative methods in science (such as accounting or experiment or simulation) answer inductively How Much. Mathematics by contrast answers deductively Why, and in a refined and philosophical version very popular among mathematicians since the early nineteenth century, Whether. "Why does a stone dropped from a tower go faster and faster?" Well, $F = ma$, understand? "I wonder Whether the mass, m, of the stone has any effect at all." Well, yes, actually it does: notice that there's a little m in the answer to the Why question.

Why/Whether is not the same question as How Much. You can know that forgetting your lover's birthday will have some effect on your relationship (Whether), and even understand that the neglect works through such-and-such an understandable psychological mechanism ("Don't you love me enough to know I *care* about birthdays?"—Why). But to know How Much the neglect will hurt the relationship you need to have in effect numbers, those ms and as, so to speak, and some notion of their magnitudes. Even if you know the Why (the proper theory of the channels through which forgetting a birthday will work; again by analogy, $F = ma$), the How Much will depend on exactly, numerically, quantitatively how sensitive this or that part of the Why is in fact in your actual beloved's soul: how much in this case the m and a are. And such sensitivity in an actual world, the scientists are always saying, is an empirical question, not theoretical. "All right, you jerk, that's the last straw: I'm moving out" or "Don't worry, dear: I know you love me" differ in the sensitivity, the How

Much, the quantitative effect, the magnitude, the mass, the oomph.

Economics since its beginning has been very often "mathematical" in this sense of being interested in Why/Whether arguments *without regard to How Much*. For example: If you buy a loaf of bread from the super-market both you and the supermarket (its shareholders, its employees, its bread suppliers) are made to some degree better off. How do I know? Because the super-market offered the bread voluntarily and you accepted the offer voluntarily. Both of you must have been made better off, a little or a lot—or else you two wouldn't have done the deal.

Economists have long been in love with this simple argument. They have since the eighteenth century taken the argument a crucial and dramatic step further: that is, they have *deduced* something from it, namely, *Free trade is neat*. If each deal between you and the supermarket, and the supermarket and Smith, and Smith and Jones, and so forth is betterment-producing (a little or a lot: we're not talking quantities here), then (note the "then": we're talking deduction here) free trade between the entire body of French people and the entire body of English people is betterment-producing, too. And therefore (note the "therefore") free trade between *any* two groups is neat. The economist notes that if all trades are voluntary they all have some gain. So free trade in all its forms is neat. For example, a law restricting who can get into the pharmacy business is a bad idea, not neat at all, because free trade is good, so non-free trade is bad. Protection of French workers is bad, because free trade is good. And so forth, to literally thousands of policy conclusions.

Though it is among the three or four most important arguments in economics, it is not empirical. It contains no statements of How Much. It says *there exists* a gain from trade—remember the phrases *some gain* or *to some degree* or *a little* or *a lot* or *we're not talking quantities here*. "I wonder Whether there exists [in *whatever* quantity] a good effect of free trade." Yes, one exists: examine this page of math; look at this diagram; listen to my charming parable about you and the supermarket. Don't ask How Much. The reasoning is Why/Whether. As stated it cannot be wrong, no more than the Pythagorean Theorem can be. It's not a matter of approximation, not a matter of How Much. It's a chain of logic from implicit axioms (which can be and have been made explicit, in all their infinite variety) to a "rigorous" *qualitative* conclusion (in *its* infinite variety). Remember those words "then," "therefore," "so." Under such-and-such a set of assumptions, *A*, the conclusion, *C*, must be that people are made better off. *A* implies *C*, so free trade is beneficial anywhere. (Please listen, and *stop* asking "How Much?": how many times must I remind you that the reasoning is qualitative, not quantitative?!)

The philosophers call this sort of thing "valid" reasoning, by which they do not mean "true," but "following from the axioms—if you believe the axioms, such as A, then C also must be true." If you believe that any individual exchange arrived at voluntarily is good, then with a few extra assumptions (e.g., about the meaning of "voluntarily"; or, e.g., about how one person's good depends on another's) you can get the conclusion that free international trade among nations is good.

Why/Whether reasoning, which is also characteristic of the Math Department, could be called philosophical. The Math Department and the Philosophy Department have a similar fascination with deduction, and a corresponding boredom with induction. They do not give a fig for How Much. No facts, please: we're philosophers. No numbers, please: we're mathematicians. In the Philosophy Department either relativism is or is not open to a refutation from self-contradiction. It's not a *little* refuted. It's knocked down, or not. In the Math Department the Goldbach Conjecture, that every even number is the sum of two prime numbers (*e.g.*, 24 = 13 + 11; try it), is either true or false (or, to introduce a third possibility admitted since the 1930s, undecidable). Supposing it's decidable, there's no question of How Much. You can't, in the realm of Why/Whether, in the Math Department or the Philosophy Department or some parts of the Economics Department, be a little bit pregnant.

The argument for free trade is easy to express in terms that anyone would call "mathematical." Since about 1947 the front line and later the dominant and by now the arrogantly self-satisfied and haughtily intolerant if remarkably unproductive scientific program in

14

economics has been to reformulate verbal (but still philosophical/mathematical, i.e. *qualitative*, i.e. Why/Whether) arguments into symbols and variables and diagrams and fixed point theorems and the like. The program is called "Samuelsonian," after the Gary, Indiana native and third person to receive the Nobel Memorial Prize in Economics, Paul Anthony Samuelson. He and his brother-in-law Kenneth Arrow (who was the fifth person out of the fifty or so from 1969 to 2001 to receive the glittering Prize) led the movement to be explicit about the math in economics, against great opposition. They were courageous pioneers (their mutual nephew Lawrence Summers, the crown prince of modern economics, became Secretary of the Treasury and President of Harvard). In 1947 Samuelson set the tone with the publication of his Ph.D. dissertation (which had been finished in 1941), the modestly entitled *Foundations of Economic Analysis*. In 1951 Arrow carried it to still higher realms of mathematics with *his* Ph.D. dissertation, *Social Choice and Individual Values*. Their enemies, a few of whom are still around, said, with the humanists, "Yuk. This math stuff is too hard, too inhuman. Give me words. Sentiment. Show me some verbal argumentation or some verbal history. Or even actual numbers. But none of this new *x* and *y* stuff. It gives me a headache."

Refutatio: But think again. There's nothing whatever new about deductive reasoning in economics. It didn't start in 1947. More like 1747 (in fact about this time David Hume in Scotland and the physiocrats in France were busy inventing philosophical, entirely qualitative,

Why/Whether arguments about economics).
Deducing sometimes surprising and anyway logically
valid (if not always true) conclusions from assumptions
about the economy is a game economists have always
loved. And if you *want* to connect one thing with
another, deduce conclusions C from assumptions A,
free trade from characterizations of an autonomous
consumer, why not do it universally and for all time?
Why not, asked Samuelson and Arrow and the rest,
with much justice, do it right?

True, for practical purposes of surveying grain fields it
would work just as well as Pythogoras' Greek proof to
have a Babylonian-style of proof-by-calculation
showing that the sums of squares of the sides of zillions
of triangles seem to be pretty much equal to the sums
of squares of their hypotenuses. You might make a
similar case for the free trade theorem, noting for
example that the great internal free-trade zone called
the United States still has a much higher average
income (20 to 30 percent higher) than otherwise clever
and hard working countries like Japan or Germany,
which insist on many more restrictions on internal
trade, such as protection of small retailing. And, true,
the improvement of computers is making more
Babylonian-style "brute force calculations" (as the
mathematicians call them with distaste) cheaper than
some elegant formulas ("analytic solutions," they say,
rapturously). Economics, like many other fields—
architecture, engineering—is about to be revolution-
ized by computation.

But if beyond clumsy fact or numerical approximation there is an elegant and exact formula—$F = ma$ or $E = mC^2$ or, to give a somewhat less elegant example from economics, $1 + i_{usa} = (e_{forward} / e_{spot}) (1 + i_{france})$, called "covered interest arbitrage"—why not use it? Of course, any deduction depends on the validity of the premises. If a sufficiently high percentage of potential arbitrageurs in the markets for French and U.S. bonds and currency are slothful dolts, then covered interest arbitrage will not hold. But likewise any *in*duction depends on the validity of the *data*. If the sample used to test the efficacy of mammograms in preventing premature death is biased, then the statistical conclusions will not hold. Any calculation depends on the validity of the inputs and assumptions. Garbage in, garbage out. As the kids say, it all depends. Naturally: we mortals are not blessed with certitude.

So mathematics, too, is not the sin of economics, but in itself a virtue. Getting deductions right is the Lord's work, if not the *only* work the Lord favors. Like all virtues it can be carried too far, and be unbalanced with other virtues, becoming the Devil's work, sin. But all virtues are like that.

Libertarian Politics

Nor is devotion to free markets a sin. Like quantitative induction and philosophical deduction, economics has always had a political purpose, and the purpose has usually been libertarian. Economists are freedom nuts, which is to say that they look with suspicion on lawyerly plans to solve problems with new state compulsions and longer jail sentences. Economics at its philosophical birth, among physiocrats in Paris and moral philosophers in Edinburgh, was in favor of free markets and was suspicious of overblown states. Mostly it still is. Let things be, *laissez faire*, has been the economists' cry against intervention. Let the trades begin.

True, not all economists are free traders. The non-free traders, often European and disproportionately nowadays French, point out that you can make other assumptions about how trade works, *A'*, and get other conclusions, *C'*, not so favorable to *laissez faire*. The free-trade theorem, which sounds so grand, is actually pretty easy to overturn. Suppose a big part of the economy—say the household—is, as the economists put it, "distorted" (e.g., suppose people in households do things for love: you can see that the economists have a somewhat peculiar idea of "distortion"). Then it follows rigorously (that is to say, mathematically) that free trade in *other* sectors (e.g., manufacturing) will *not* be the best thing. In fact it can make the average person worse off than restricted, protected, tariffed trade would.

And of course normal people—I mean non-economists—are not persuaded that free trade is always and everywhere a good thing. For example most people think free trade is a bad thing for the product or service *they* make. By all means, let us arrange for my baker and pharmacist to compete vigorously, nay, brutally, with other bakers and pharmacists, so that I can get donuts and also vitamin E (to offset the donuts) cheaply. But I really do think we need to blockade entry into the profession of being an economist: it is, I am sure you agree, scandalous that so many unqualified quacks are bilking consumers with adulterated economics, quite unlike the pure economic ideas I offer here, at such reasonable expense.

And very many normal people of leftish views, even after communism, even after numerous disastrous experiments in central planning, even after trying to get a train ride from Amtrak or service from the Postal Service (not to mention service from the Internal Revenue Service or from the Immigration and Naturalization Service; you see I wax indignant: I am, after all, a free-market economist), think Socialism Deserves a Chance. They think it obvious that socialism is after all fairer than unfettered capitalism. They think it obvious that regulation is after all necessary to restrain monopoly. They don't realize that free markets have partially broken down inequality (for example, between men and women; "partially," I said) and partially undermined monopolies (for example, local monopolies in retailing) and have increased the income of the poor over two centuries by a factor of 18. The sin of economics, the lefties think, is exactly its free-market bias.

Refutatio: But, my dearly beloved friends on the left,

think, think again. There really is a serious case to be made against government intervention and in favor of markets. Maybe not knockdown; maybe imperfect here or there; let's chat about it; hmm, I see what you mean; but a serious case that serious people ought to take seriously. The case is *not* merely Country-Club Republicanism (which in fact is highly favorable to government intervention, in order you see to assist the members of the Country Club, such as its longstanding members who managed Enron, Inc.). The case in favor of markets is on the contrary populist and egalitarian and person-respecting and bad-institution-breaking libertarianism. Don't go to government to solve problems, said Adam Smith. As he didn't say, to do so is to put the fox in charge of the hen house. The golden rule is, those who have the gold rule: so don't expect a government run by men to help women, or a government run by Enron executives to help Enron employees.

Libertarianism is typical of economics, especially English-speaking economics, and most especially American economics. Most Americans if they can get clear of certain European errors, are radical libertarians under the skin. Give me liberty. Sweet land of liberty. Live free or die (a New Hampshire man who decided he didn't want the motto on his license plate and insisted on covering it up with masking tape was... arrested: your friend the State in action).

But alas, no time, no time. Libraries of books have been written examining the numerous and weighty arguments for the market and against socialism. I urge you to go read a few such books with care, such as Thomas Friedman, *The Lexus and the Olive Tree*, or if your tastes run more academic, anything by Milton Friedman (Nobel 1976). Please, all of you, come over to my delightful, if challenging, course at the University of Illinois - Chicago called "Economics for Advanced Students of the Humanities" in which I sketch the arguments. Really, that the average literary person believes the first few pages of *The Communist Manifesto* suffice for knowledge of economics and economic history, in which he professes great interest, is a bit of a scandal. It's amazing that most professors and journalists since about 1900 have not even *heard* of the arguments against turning the economy over to police and jailers and bureaucrats, and are scandalized when some boorish Chicago-School economist comes along and suggests that pot should be legalized and national borders opened and government schools made to compete with each other. I spoiled quite a few dinner parties early in my career blurting out such proposals. I have become cannier since then, or more polite, or just weary.

But I say, as Cromwell said wearily to the General Assembly of the Church of Scotland, 3 August, 1650, "I beseech you, in the bowels of Christ, think it possible you may be mistaken."

Oh, permit me one short libertarian riff. According to the Peruvian development economist Hernando de Soto, to open a small business in Lima, Peru getting all the forms filled out and visiting the right government offices recently took a team of researchers working six hours a day *289 days*. To get the permits to build a legal house on state-owned land (land for sale, not held for the public) took nearly *7 years*, with 207 administrative steps and 52 government offices. In Egypt getting the permits to build a legal house on agricultural land took from *6 to 11 years*. In Haiti buying land from the government took *19 years*.

Nor is such government obstruction peculiar to the present-day Third World. In one decade in the eighteenth century, according to the Swedish economist and historian Eli Heckscher in his book of 1932, *Mercantilism*, the French government sent tens of thousands of souls to the galleys *and executed 16,000* (that's about 4.4 people a day over the ten years: you see the beauty of statistical thinking) for the hideous crime of... are you ready to hear the appalling evil these enemies of the State committed, fully justifying hanging them all, every damned one of their treasonable skins? *...importing printed calico cloth*. States do not change much from age to age. Lawrence Wylie reported the attitude of a French bureaucrat in the 1950s: "If the public speaks evil of me I serenely shit on it. The complaint merely goes to show the value of my office and of my methods. The more the public is shat upon, the better the State is served."

In view of How Muches and Oh, My Gods like these— the baleful oomph of governmental intrusions worldwide crushing harmless (indeed, beneficial) exchange, from marijuana to printed calico—perhaps *laissez faire* does not seem so obviously sinful, does it now? Consider, my dear leftist friends. Read and reflect. I beseech you, think it possible that, like statistics and mathematics, the libertarianism of economics is a virtue.

VENIAL SINS, EASILY FORGIVEN

I am very far from wanting to defend everything about economics, even short of the Two Great Secret Sins. But you need to realize that economists do the irritating things they do for reasons, often pretty good ones.

For instance, among the most surprising and irritating features of economics (when people figure out what is going on) is its obsessive, monomaniacal focus on a Prudent model of humanity. It's hard for outsiders to believe. Everything, simply everything, from marriage to murder is supposed by the modern economist to be explainable as a sort of Prudence. Human beings are supposed to be calculating machines pursuing Prudence and Price and Profit and Property and Power—"*P* variables," you might call them. *P*-obsession begins with Machiavelli and Hobbes, is continued by Bernard Mandeville (the early eighteenth-century Dutch-English spy and pamphleteer), is systematized by Jeremy Bentham (the utilitarian economist flourishing in the early nineteenth century), and is finally perfected by twentieth-century economists, including that same

Paul Samuelson (b. 1915), who fully formalized the notion in a curious character known as Max U, and the great Gary Becker (b. 1930), who went about as far as he could go.

Becker (Nobel 1992), a professor of economics and sociology at the University of Chicago, asks, for example, why people have children. Answer: *because children are durable goods.* They are expensive to produce and maintain, over a long period of time, like a house. They yield returns over a long future, like a car. They have a poor second-hand market, like a refriger-ator. They act as a store of value against future disas-ters, like pawnable gold or your diamond ring. So (you will sense a logical leap here; David Hume noticed the same leap in Mandeville and Hobbes), the number of children that people have is a matter of cost and benefit, just like the purchase of a house or car or refrigerator or diamond. A prudent parent decides whether to invest in many children or few, extensively or intensively, early or late, just like investing in a durable good.

If you think this is funny stuff you are not alone. But think again: there's no doubt that Prudence does affect at least part of the decision to have children, to emigrate, to attend church, to go to college, to commit a murder, not to speak of buying a house or a car or a loaf of bread. In his obsessive study of the Prudential part, the economist can make some quite interesting and sometimes counter-intuitive and occasionally even factually true points. For example, economists "predict" (as they always put it in their child's version of positivism) that, surprisingly, no-fault divorce should have no long-term effect on the prevalence of divorce. Why is that? Well, the law affects how the spoils from a divorce are divided up, but *not their total size*. Since the people on both sides have lawyers paid to collect spoils, it is the *sum* of spoils, not their division, which should in fact determine how much divorcing goes on. That the wife gets half instead of one quarter is offset by the necessary concomitant: the husband therefore gets half instead of three-quarters. Her increasing propensity to seek divorce (half is better than one quarter) is offset by his decreasing propensity (a half is worse than three quarters). And such a surprising claim on the basis of Prudence alone seems to be factually true in the world.

The narrowness of the scientific concern of economists has of course a cost (which is itself an economist's point: the road not traveled is the opportunity cost). Prudence is the central ethical virtue of the bourgeoisie, but not the only one. Adam Smith's book about Prudence, *An Inquiry into the Nature and Causes of the Wealth of Nations*, published in 1776, should be read as embedded in the other virtues, especially Temperance and Justice, about which indeed Smith wrote at great length. If Smith had been statistically inclined then he would have put it this way. Take any sort of behavior you wish to understand—voting, for example, or the adoption of the Bessemer process in the making of steel. Call it *B*. It can be put on a scale and measured, or perhaps seen to be present or absent.

You want to give an account of B. What the Prudence-Only men from Machiavelli to Becker are claiming is that you can explain B with Prudence alone, the P variable—Prudence, Price, Profit, The Profane. Smith (and Mill and Keynes and quite a few other economists, if not the ones who run the discipline these days) have replied that, no, you have forgotten Love and Courage, Justice and Temperance, Faith and Hope, in a word, Solidarity, the S variable of speech, stories, shame, The Sacred. Economists have specialized in P, anthropologists in S. But most behavior, B, is explained by both:

$$B = a + \beta P + yS + \varepsilon.$$

To include both P and S is only sensible. It is not wishy-washy or unprincipled. Of course the S variables are the conditions under which the P variables work, and of course the P variables modify the effects of S variables. It is the human dance of Sacred and Profane.

(Econometrically speaking, I remind my economist colleagues, if the P and S variables are not orthogonal, which is to say if they are not entirely independent, or the covariance, as we say, of P and S is not zero, by God's grace, bless her holy name, or alternatively if there is reason to believe that a variable such as PS multiplied together (say) has its own influence, then an estimate of the coefficients a and β that ignores S (or PS) will give biased results. The bias is important if the S variable is important. The experiment is not properly controlled, and its conclusions are nonsense.)

It is often a mistake to rely on S alone, and to reject P, as Marshall Sahlins sometimes seems to do (shame on you, Marshall; he says he doesn't, but I say he does). And vice versa, which is the point here. Most economics and most anthropology is persuasion about the mixture of Prudence and Solidarity, the Profane and the Sacred, that matters for any particular case. Without being explicit enough, some economists, and some of the best, do acknowledge S variables. Theodore Schultz argued in *Transforming Traditional Agriculture* (1964; Nobel 1979) that peasants in poor countries were Prudent. He was arguing that it was a mistake to explain their behavior anthropology-style as $B = a + yS + E$ with the S variable alone. Schultz said: Even these "traditional" peasants care about P. But Schultz did not ignore the S variables. The education of women, he argued forcefully, was crucial in making Prudence work, and doing it would depend on over-coming patriarchal objections to literate women. Robert Fogel (Nobel 1993) and Stanley Engerman argued in 1974 that American slavery was Prudential and capitalistic. But they did not entirely ignore the S variables. They measured them, by indirection, finding that for some features of slavery, such as the price of slaves, variables other than business Prudence were quantitatively not very important. And then Fogel went on to write about the influence of religious belief on slavery and abolition, and Engerman to write about the historical roots of coercion and freedom in the labor market. Many economists go through a *Bildung* of this sort, starting in graduate school as Prudence-Only guys (the guys more than the gals) and coming by age 50 or so to realize that, after all, people are motivated by more than Prudence. Even Gary Becker shows signs of such a development.

To this the academic economist who has *not* developed beyond his graduate-student version of the science is likely to reply, following the *P*-Only model, "Thanks for the advice. But I make a good living specializing in *P* variables." His sin is a selfish species of Ivory-Towerism. "Why do I need to concern myself with the *entire* argument? I do my specialty."

Well, so what? Don't you want to get the correct answer; or do you merely want to collect your paycheck? (Don't answer that.)

NUMEROUS WEIGHTY SINS REQUIRING SPECIAL GRACE TO FORGIVE BUT SINS NOT PECULIAR TO ECONOMICS

And then there are sins less easily forgiven, less easily put down to a prudent specialization that at least keeps *P* variables in the scientific game. The sins are shameful and scientifically damaging, I admit, having myself committed all of them at one time or another, sometimes for years and years. I am truly sorry and I humbly repent. But, goodness, if you are going to damn economics for *these* you are going to have to line up for damnation a considerable portion of the intelligentsia, commencing probably with your own sweet self.

Economists, for example, are *Institutionally Ignorant*, which is to say that they don't have much curiosity about the world they are trying to explain. For example—this will surprise you—academic economists, especially since Samuelsonianism took over, have come to think it is simply irrelevant, a waste of time, to do actual field work in the businesses they talk about. This is because (as they will explain to you patiently) *people might lie*, a point which is taken among economists to be a profound remark in proper scientific method. So (you will see the *non sequitur*) never ask a businessperson why she does something. Just observe, as though people were ants. The great economist Ronald Coase (also at the University of Chicago, Nobel 1991, but taking a different approach to *P* and *S* than Gary Becker does—Coase is no Samuelsonian), while still a student at the London School of Economics, had the startling idea of *actually speaking* to businesspeople. He has been trying ever since about October 1932 to get other economists to do the same thing. No soap. When two economists, Arjo Klamer and David Colander, asked economics graduate students what the skills were that made for a good economist, nearly two thirds named mathematical ability and the ability to think up quick little models of Prudence Only. How many named *knowledge of the economic world* as important? Go ahead, guess.

About three-and-a-half percent.

The figure was so shocking even to economists that it became part of an investigation into graduate programs by the American Economic Association. Reform was blocked by a member of the committee, also at the University of Chicago (are you seeing a pattern here?), who wants the math-with-Prudence-Only game to go on and on, undisturbed by scientific considerations.

Outsiders would likewise be amazed at the *Historical Ignorance* of the economist. They think that the scientific evidence about economies before the past few years would surely figure in an economist's data. It doesn't. One graduate program after another in the 1970s and 1980s cut the requirement that students become familiar with the economic past. I myself managed for twelve years to fend off the day of execution at the University of Chicago (*now* do you see the pattern?). The very month I left the department in disgust the barbarians inside the gates sent the economic history requirement to the guillotine, and since then Ph.D.s in economics from the University of Chicago have joined those at Minnesota, Princeton, and Columbia in ignorance of the economic past. At the same time almost all American graduate programs (my own fair Harvard was proudly among the first to do so) were abandoning the study of the past of economics itself. People call themselves economists who have never read a page of Adam Smith or Karl Marx or John Maynard Keynes. It would be like being an anthropologist who had never heard of Malinowski or an evolutionary biologist who had never heard of Darwin.

The more general *Cultural Barbarism* of economists is well illustrated by their *Philosophical Naïveté*. Few economists read outside economics. It is unnerving to gaze about the library of a distinguished professor of economics and find no books at all except on applied math and statistics: these are the worldly philosophers who run our nation? Uh-oh. So naturally the professors of economics have childish ideas about, say, epistemology. They think for example that early logical positivism (c. 1920), misunderstood because received third or fourth hand, is the latest philosophical word on meaningfulness. "Let's see now: I think I can recall from my high school physics course. If a Hypothesis, *H*, does not imply materially observable Observations, *O*, then it is 'meaningless,' right? So that means... 'means'? Uh... well, let it go... that all ethics, introspections, accounts of mental states, metaphors, frames of meaning, literature and myths—and it would seem all of mathematics and philosophy itself, I guess; but *that* can't be right—are meaningless blabber. Hmm. There must be something wrong here. Well, good enough for government work."

The economists know nothing of the main finding of linguistics, philosophy, and literary criticism in the twentieth century, namely, that we have ways of world making, language games, senses of an ending that cannot be reduced to formal grammars, even in prin-

ciple (economists have themselves stumbled on analo-
gous findings in their own highly non-humanistic work,
such as the finding of "rational expectations" or "the
cheap talk paradox"). A famous story in linguistics
illustrates the point. A very pompous linguist was
giving a talk at Columbia and noted that there were
languages in which a double negative meant a positive
(standard English, for example: "I am not going to not
speak" = "I am going to speak") and languages in which
a double negative is a stronger negative (standard
French and Italian, for example; or non-standard
English: "You ain't got no class"). But, says he, articulating what he imagined was a universal of grammar,
"There are no languages in which a double *positive* is a
negative." Pause. Silence. Then came a loud and
knowing sneer from the back of the room: "Yeah,
yeah."

Their high-school version of positivism means the
economists depend on a *high-school version of the philosophy of science.* "Well, you see: if *H* implies *O*, then it
follows rigorously that not-*O* implies not-*H*. So I can
falsify a hypothesis simply by looking at the observable
implications, *O*. What a wonderful simplification of
my obligation to make scientific arguments! I can test
the hypothesis that people vote their pocketbooks, for
example, just by looking at how a party's platform
would affect voter Smith or Jones in their pocketbooks.
And if it's not so falsified, it's confirmed, right?"

Never mind that Pierre Duhem pointed out as long
ago as 1906 that the argument is nonsense in actual

science because every experiment or observation has scientific controls (for example, S variables; or measuring devices and measuring errors) the truth or irrelevance of which needs to be assumed to make the test work. (Economists call this the specification problem.) So the specification is actually H _and_ S_1 _and_ S_2 _and_ S_3 _and_... implies _not-O_ _or_ _not-S_1 _or_ _not-S_2 _or_ _not-S_3 _or_ ....This means that the "falsifying" observation may actually be a result of some failure of experimental control. And in fact on the frontiers of science the most usual quarrels are about just such matters: have you failed to control properly? Is your specification right? Is it rational to expect people to be rational in a voting booth when they have already shown their irrationality by showing up at the polls in the first place, considering that their (or rather, his or her) single vote is virtually certain not to change the outcome? Have you properly controlled for social solidarity and sentiment and other S variables affecting the vote, and are these uncorrelated with the included variable, P, the pocketbook effect?

The words "metaphysical" or "philosophical" are used in economics nowadays as terms of contempt: "That's rather _philosophical_, isn't it?" means, "What a stupid, unscientific point; only an English professor would say such a thing!" So not surprisingly economists adhere without criticism to, for instance, _a high-school version of ethical philosophy_. Economists believe that scientific and ethical questions are distinct, the one "positive" and the other "normative," and that real scientists ought to (hmm...) stick to the positive. I know it's hard to believe, but most economists really do think that the positive/normative distinction lets them out of any reflection on ethics. They want to believe that: "Economics is like astronomy in having nothing to do with human affairs and therefore with the ethical universe in which humans live. No, wait, that can't be right: it has to do with human affairs—how else am I going to get paid for consulting or editorializing?—but the parts I deal with are Objective... like who gets hurt by the imposition of free trade. Hmm. I'm having trouble with this. What I'm sure of is that 'ought' and 'is' are entirely different realms and the scientist ought to ignore... uhm... well...."

And economists are tempted to *arrogance in social engineering*. Most humanists do not face the problem, since poets seldom think to ask English professors how to write poems—though of course "criticism" in the belletristic, three-star-awarding, judgments-of-Greatness sense does face the temptation, and normally yields to it; and in fact many poets *have* been influenced by criticism (Poe's criticism inspired Baudelaire; Emerson's inspired Whitman). Anthropologists know about the problem in their own work, and worry: am I becoming a tool of Western imperialism?

Since economists think themselves well informed about ethical philosophy if they have a muddy understanding of positive vs. normative, you can imagine the results. I would not want to accuse my colleagues of being engineers devising efficiently operating exter-

mination chambers. At least not often. The libertarian streak in economics sometimes stays their hand.
An economist would not view poor people as cattle to
be herded into high-rise concentration camps—as
architects in the 1950s, for example, demonstrably
did; and as D. H. Lawrence and other democracy-
haters earlier did. Or would they? What ethical
consideration would stop them?

And economists are prone to an odd personality
defect arising from their *P*-Only models, *candid selfishness*. When you ask a Chicago-School economist,
"George, would you cooperate on this?" he is liable to
answer, "No: it's not in my self-interest: don't you
believe in economics?" When I left Chicago so long
ago one of these people came up to me and said, "I
suppose you aren't going to help grade the core examination—after all, you're out of here." I was astonished, and replied, "No, I'm going to fulfill my
remaining obligations." He in turn was astonished. I
do not think it raised his opinion of me, that I was so
inconsistent in advocating a *P*-Only theory in
economic history (as I was then) but not in everyday
life. You mean you *don't* cheat your employer when
you get a chance? You mean you *don't* impose
burdens on your colleagues when it serves your
narrow interests? Huh? What kind of an economist
are you?

And I have to mention finally the very widespread
opinion that economists are prone to the sin of
pride—*personal arrogance*. Some names that come up

in this connection are: Paul Krugman (gold medal in this category), Robert Lucas (Nobel 1995), and Deirdre McCloskey (bronze). Lots of intellectual professions are arrogant. Physicists, for example, are contemptuous of chemists, whom they regard as imperfect versions of themselves. In fact physicists are contemptuous of most people. But when a physicist at North Carolina named Robert Palmer went in 1989 to a conference in which physicists and economists were to educate each other he remarked, "I used to think that physicists were the most arrogant people in the world. The economists were, if anything, more arrogant." I'm afraid he's right on this score. Though of course in general he's a dope: a mere *physicist*.

Apologia: I have not, I realize, painted a very attractive picture of economics. But these sins are widespread, I repeat, among non-economists, too—even that odd one, *candid selfishness*, which you can find Nature's Economists articulating even when they aren't trained in it. But I earnestly invite you to learn by further reading in the literature the offsetting merits of economists:

Economists are for one thing serious about the public interest, and are often the only people defending it with any sort of lucidity and persuasiveness against the special interests. The model of worldly philosophy was originated in crude form by the early pamphleteers and political arithmeticians (among them Daniel Defoe). Adam Smith a half century and more later brought it to perfection.

And if you like engineers you will like many economists. Engineers are attractive people, hard working (you have to be hard working to absorb all that engineering math), earnest and practical, bent always on Solving the Problem. True, they are often simple-minded. But simplicity gets the job done. Lots of economists are engineering types.

Or lawyer types. Like lawyers the economists are good arguers, which is good when you need a good argument ("How do you want it to come out?"). Economists can debate each other and yet not lose their tempers and not make irrelevant appeals to rank. Economists like lawyers are clear-minded, professionally. They are used to getting to the point and staying there. The humor of economists, unhappily, is often cynical, as it is also among lawyers, seldom generous, but *that's* true in many fields of the intellect.

But, above all, economics is about important matters. It would be remarkable if the economics-since-Marx that most non-economists would rather not read had *nothing* worthwhile in it. After all, thousands of apparently intelligent (they certainly think so) economists have labored away at it now for a century and a half.

I beseech you, dear reader, think it possible that economists, even Chicago-School economists, even Samuelsonian economists, have some important things to say about the economy.

THE TWO REAL SINS, ALMOST PECULIAR TO ECONOMICS

A real science, or any intelligent inquiry into the world, whether the study of earthquakes or the study of poetry, economics or physics, history or anthropology, art history or organic chemistry, a systematic inquiry into one's lover or a systematic inquiry into the Dutch language, must do two things. If it only does one of them it is not an inquiry into the world. It may be good in some other way, but not in the double way that we associate with good science or other good inquiries into the world, such as a detective solving a case.

I am sure you will agree: An inquiry into the world must think and it must look. It must theorize and must observe. Formalize and record. Both. That's obvious and elementary. Not everyone involved in a *collective* intelligent inquiry into the world need do both: the detective can assign his dim-witted assistant to just observe. But the inquiry as a whole must reflect and must listen. Both. Of course.

Pure thinking, such as mathematics or philosophy, is not, however, to be disdained, not at all. Euler's equation, $e^{\pi i} + 1 = 0$, really is quite remarkable, linking "the five most important constants in the whole of analysis" (as Philip Davis and Reuben Hersh note), and would be a remarkable cultural achievement even if it had no worldly use. But certainly the equation is not a result of *looking* at the world. So it is not science; it is a kind of abstract art. Mathematicians are proud of the uselessness of most of what they do, as well they might be: Mozart is "useless," too; to what would you "apply" the Piano Sonata in A? I have a brilliant and learned friend who is an intellectual historian of note. He and I were walking to lunch in Iowa City one day and I said offhandedly, assuming he would of course know this, that mathematics was one of the great achievements of Western culture. He was so astonished by the claim that he stopped short and argued with me there on the sidewalk by the Old Capitol Mall: "Surely math is like plumbing: useful, but hardly in touch with deeper things; hardly a *cultural* achievement!" I tried to persuade him that he felt this way only because he had no acquaintance with mathematics, but I don't think I succeeded.

Nor is pure, untheorized observation to be disdained. There is something in narration, for example, that is untheorizable (though it is surprising to non-humanists how much of it *can* and has recently been theorized by literary critics). At some level a story is just a story, and artful choice of detail within the story is sheer observation—not *brute* observation, which is a hopeless ambition to record *everything*, but sheer. I have another brilliant and learned friend, an economist, who tells the story of how as a boy in Amsterdam he decided one day to embark in all seriousness on Social Observation. He was about ten years old when this ambition overcame him, so he equipped himself with a notebook and a pen and went to a big street and started to, well, observe. He decided to note down the license number of every car that passed. For many hours he kept it up, thrilled to be at last a real observer of society. But of course when he got home and looked at the results it occurred to him that the data were meaningless. They were brute facts unshaped by any meaningful human question, or emotion, or interest. One wishes every scholar learned this at ten years old.

So pure mathematics, pure philosophy, the pure writing of pure fictions, the pure painting of pictures, the pure composing of sonatas are all, when done well or at least interestingly, admirable activities. I have to keep saying "pure" because of course it is entirely possible—indeed commonplace—for novelists, say, to take a scientific view of their subjects (Balzac, Zola, and Sinclair Lewis among many others are well known for their self-conscious practice of a scientific literature; Roman satire is another case; or Golden Age Dutch painting). Likewise scientists use elements of pure narration (in evolutionary biology and economic history) or elements of pure mathematics (in physics and economics) to make scientific arguments. I do not want to get entangled in the apparently hopeless task of solving what is known as the Demarcation Problem, discerning a line between science and other activities. It is doubtful such a line exists. The efforts of many intelligent philosophers of science appear to have gotten exactly nowhere in solving it. I am merely suggesting that a science *like many other human practices* such as knitting or making a friend should be about the world, which means it should attend to the world. And it should also be something other than miscellaneous

facts, such as the classification of animals in the *Chinese
Celestial Emporium of Benevolent Knowledge* noted by
Borges: (a.) those that belong to the Emperor, (b.)
embalmed ones, (c.) those that are trained, (d.) suckling
pigs, (e.) mermaids, and so forth, down to (n.) those
that resemble flies from a distance. Not brute facts.
And not mere theory.

So I am not dragging economics over to some implau-
sible definition of Science and then convicting it of not
corresponding to the definition. Such a move is
common in economic methodology—for example in
some of the less persuasive writings of the very persuasive economist Marc Blaug. I am merely saying that
economists want to be involved in an intelligent inquiry
into the world. If so, the field as a whole must theorize
and observe. Both. This is not controversial.

An economist at a leading graduate program listening to
me will now burst out with: "Great! I *entirely* agree:
theorize and observe, though of course as you admit we
can specialize in one or the other as long as the whole
field does both. *And that, Deirdre, is exactly what we
already do*, on a massive scale. And we do it very well, if
I don't say so myself. We do very sophisticated mathematical theorizing, such as in the Mas-Collel,
Whinston, and Green textbook (1995), and then we test
the theory in the world using very tricky econometrics,
such as Jeffrey M. Wooldridge, *Econometric Analysis of
Cross Section and Panel Data* (2001). You can see the
results in any journal of economics. Some of it is pure
theory, some econometrics. Theorize and observe."

To which I say: Bosh. *She and her colleagues, when they are being most highbrow and Science-proud, don't really do* either *theorizing or observing.* Economics in its most prestigious and academically published versions engages in two activities, *qualitative theorems* and *statistical significance*, which *look* like theorizing and observing, and have (apparently) the same tough math and tough statistics that actual theorizing and actual observing would have. *But neither of them is what it claims to be.* Qualitative theorems are not theorizing in a sense that would have to do with a double-virtued inquiry into the world. In the same sense, statistical significance is not observing.

This is the double-formed and secret sin, and this the moment:

> *Eve*
> *Intent now wholly on her taste, naught else*
> *Regarded, such delight till then, as seemed,*
> *In fruit she never tasted, whether true*
> *Or fancied so, through expectation high*
> *Of knowledge, nor was godhead from her thought.*

It is not difficult to explain to outsiders what is so dramatically, insanely, sinfully wrong with the two leading methods in high-level economics, qualitative theorems and statistical significance. It is *very* difficult to explain it to insiders, because the insiders cannot believe that methods in which they have been elaborately trained and which are used by the people they admire most are simply unscientific nonsense, having

literally nothing to do with whatever actual scientific
contribution (and I repeat, it is considerable) that
economics makes to the understanding of society. So
they simply can't grasp arguments that are plain to
people not socialized in economics. (Bibliographical
note to the insiders and the more adventuresome of the
outsiders: Chapters 10-13 in *Knowledge and Persuasion
in Economics* [1994] and Chapters 7 and 8 in *The
Rhetoric of Economics* [2nd ed. 1998]).

Hear, oh outsiders. I've told you how popular *qualitative*, Why/Whether reasoning is in economics. It takes
this form: *A* implies *C*. Got it? Simple, huh? The
crucial point is that the *A* and the *C* are indeed qualitative. They are not of the form "*A is* '4.8798'." They
are of the *qualitative* form, "*A* is 'everyone is motivated
by *P*-Only considerations'," say, which implies "free
trade is neat." No numbers. You realize your lover
will be annoyed by the neglected birthday *to some
degree*, but we're not talking about magnitudes.
Why/Whether. Not How Much. The economic
"theorists" focus on what mathematicians call "existence theorems." With such and such general (or not
so general, but anyway non-quantitative) assumptions *A*
there exists a state of the imagined world *C*. A typical
statement in economic "theory" is, "if information is
symmetric, an equilibrium of the game exists" or, "if
people are rational in their expectations in the
following sense, buzz, buzz, buzz, *then* there exists an
equilibrium of the economy in which government
policy is useless."

Okay, now imagine an *alternative* set of assumptions (like the ones used earlier to "disprove" the Free Trade Theorem), A'. Look at that last item closely. If you're going to venture into the wonderful world of this really tough, macho math we economists deal in daily you are going to have to train yourself to look closely at symbols: notice that the alternative assumption has a little mark just after it, not in math called a "single quotation mark" but a "prime" (it's just a notation to distinguish one set of things—in this case assumptions—from another; it has nothing to do with prime numbers). A' is read "A prime." Naturally, if you change assumptions (introducing households who do not operate on P-Only motivations, say; or [I speak now to insiders] making information a little asymmetric; or [ditto] introduce any Second Best, such as monopoly or taxation; or [ditto] nonconvexities in production) in general the conclusion is going to change.

Natch. There's nothing deep or surprising about this: changing your assumptions changes your conclusions. Call the new conclusion C' (a test of whether you're paying attention, class: How is it read? Answer: "C single prime"). So we have the old A implies C and the fresh, publishable novelty, A' implies C'. But, as the mathematicians say, we can add *another* prime and proceed as before, introducing some other plausible possibility for the assumptions, A'' (read it "A double prime"), which implies its own C''. And so forth: A''' implies C'''. And on and on and on and on, until the economists get tired and go home.

What has been gained by all this? It is pure thinking, philosophy. It is not disciplined by any simultaneous inquiry into How Much. It's qualitative, not quantitative, and not organized to allow quantities into the story. It's like stopping with the conclusion that forgetting your lover's birthday will have *some* bad effect on one's relationship—you still have no idea How Much, whether trivial or disastrous or somewhere in between. *So the pure thinking is unbounded.* It's a game of imagining how your lover will react *endlessly.* True, if you had good ideas about what were plausible assumptions to make, derived from some inquiry into the actual state of the world, the situation might be rescued for science and other inquiries into the world, such as the inquiry into the probably quantitative effect of missing a birthday on your lover's future commitment to you. But if not—and I'm telling you that such is the usual practice of "theoretical" pieces in economics, about half the items in any self-respecting journal of economic science—it's "just" an intellectual game.

I have expressed admiration for pure mathematics and for Mozart's concertos. Fine. But *economics is supposed to be an inquiry into the world, not pure thinking.* (If it *is* to be justified as pure thinking, just "fun," it is not very entertaining. No one would buy tickets to listen to a "theory" seminar in economics. Believe me on this one: as mathematical entertainment the stuff is *really* crummy.) The A-prime/C-prime, existence-theorem, qualitative-only "work" that economists do is like chess problems. Chess problems usually do not have anything to do even with playing real chess (since the situations are often ones that could not arise in a real game). And chess itself has nothing to do with living, except for its no doubt wonderful purity as thought, *á la* Mozart.

What kind of theory would actually contribute to a double-virtued inquiry into the world? Obviously, it would be the kind of theory for which actual numbers can conceivably be assigned. If Force equals Mass times Acceleration then you have a *potentially quantitative* insight into the flight of cannon balls, say. But the *qualitative* theorems (explicitly advocated in Samuelson's great work of 1947, and thenceforth proliferating endlessly in the professional journals of academic economics) don't have any place for actual numbers. So the "results" keep flip-flopping, endlessly, pointlessly.

The history of economic "theory" since 1947 (and, as I said, in non-mathematical form since 1747, too) is replete with examples. Samuelson himself famously showed in the 1940s that "factor prices" (such as wages) are "equalized" by trade in steel and wheat and so forth—as a qualitative theorem, under such and such assumptions, *A*. It *could* be an argument against free trade. But shortly afterwards it was shown (by Samuelson himself, among others) that if you make alternative assumptions, *A'*, you get very different conclusions. And so it went, and goes, with the limit achieved only in boredom, all over economics. Make thus-and-such assumptions, *A*, about the following game-theoretic model and you can show that a group of unsocialized individuals will form a civil society. Make another set of assumptions, A', and they won't. And so on and so forth. Blah, blah, blah, blah, to no scientific end.

Such stuff has taken over fields near to economics, first political science and now increasingly sociology. A typical "theoretical" paper in the *American Political Science Review* shows that under assumptions A the comity of nations is broken; in the next issue someone will show that under A' it is preserved. This is not theory in the sense that, say, physics uses the term. Pick up a copy of the *Physical Review* (it comes in four versions; pick any). Open it at random. You will find mind-breakingly difficult math, and physics that no one except a specialist in the particular tiny field can follow. But always, on every page, you will find repeated, persistent attempts to *answer the question How Much*. Go ahead: do it. Don't worry; it doesn't matter that you can't understand the physics. You will see that the physicists use in nearly every paragraph a rhetoric of How Much. Even the theorists as against the experimenters in physics spend their days trying to figure out ways of calculating *magnitudes*. The give-away that something other than scientific is going on in "theoretical" economics (and, alas, political science) is that it contains not, from beginning to end of the article, a single attempt at a magnitude.

So: Secret Sin Number One: qualitative theorems.

"But wait a minute, Deirdre," the Insider Economist breaks in (he is getting very, very annoyed because, as I told you, he Just Doesn't Get It). "You admitted that we economists also do econometrics, that is, formal testing of economic hypotheses using advanced statistical theory. You, as an economist, can hardly object to specialization: some people do theory, some empirical work."

Yes, my dear young colleague. Since I have been to your house and noted that you have not a single work on economics before your own graduate training I suppose you are not aware that the argument was first made explicit in 1957 by Tjalling Koopmans, a Dutch-American economist at Yale (Nobel 1975), who in his *Three Essays on the State of Economic Science* recommended just such a specialization. He recommended that "theorists" spend their time on gathering a "card file" of qualitative theorems attaching a sequence of axioms A', A'', A''', etc. to a sequence of conclusions C', C', C''', etc., *separated from* the empirical work, "for the protection [note the word, students of free trade] of both."

Now this would be fine if the theorems were not qualitative. If they took the form that theorems do in physics (better called "derivations," since physicists are completely uninterested in the existence theorems that obsess mathematicians and philosophers), good. Then the duller wits like Deirdre McCloskey the economic historian could be assigned to mere observation, filling in blanks in the theory. *But there are no blanks to fill in*, no How Much questions asked, in the theory that economists admire the most and that has taken over half of their waking hours.

Still, things would not be so bad, so sunk in scientific sin, if on the lower-status empirical side of academic economics all was well. The empiricists like me in their dull-witted way could cobble together actual scientific hypotheses, simply ignoring the "work" of the qualitative theorists. Actual players of chess could ignore the "results" from chess problems. In effect this is what happens. The "theories" proffered by the "theorists" are not tested. In their stead linearized models that try crudely to control for this or that effect are used. An empiricist could therefore try to extract the world's information about the price sensitivity of demand for housing in Britain in the 1950s, say.

But the sin is double. The empirical economists *also* have become confused by qualitative "results." *They, too,* have turned away from one of the two questions necessary for a serious inquiry into the world (the other is Why), How Much. The sin sounds improbable, since empirical economics is drenched in numbers, but the numbers they acquire with their most sophisticated tools (as against their most common tools, such as simple enumeration and systems of accounting) are it turns out meaningless.

The confusion and meaninglessness arises from a particular technique in statistical studies, called "statistical significance." It has become since the cheapening of computation in the 1970s a plague in economics, in psychology, and, most alarmingly, in medical science. Consider the decades-long dispute over the prescribing of routine mammograms to screen for early forms of breast cancer. One school says, Start at age 40. The other says, No, age 50. (And still another, Never routinely. But set that aside.) Why do they differ? The American nurses' epidemiological study or the Swedish studies on which the empirical arguments are based are quite large. But there's a lot of what engineers call "noise" in the data, lots of things going on. So: although starting as early as age 40 does seem to have *some* effect, the samples are not large enough to be conclusive. By what standard? By the standard called "statistical significance [at the 5%, 1%, 0.1%, or whatever level]." The medical statisticians will be glad to explain to you (for example, the over-50 school will) that "significance" in this narrow and technical sense of the word tells you how likely it is the result comes just from the noise. A "highly" significant result is one in which the sample is large enough to overwhelm the noise. That is, it's unlikely—those 5%, 1%, etc. figures, successively more stringent—you'll be fooled into thinking there's an effect when in fact the effect in the real world is zero.

So the situation is this. The over-50 school admits that there is *some* positive effect in detecting early cancers from starting mammograms as early as age 40; but, they say with a sneer, it's *uncertain*. You'll be taking some chance of being fooled by chance. Nasty business. Really, something to avoid.

Huh? Are you telling me, Mr. Medical Statistician, that even though there is a life-saving effect of early mammograms in the data on average, *you are uncomfortable about claiming it?* I thought the purpose of medical research was to save lives. Your comfort is not, as I understand it, what we are chiefly concerned with. You find the data noisy. I'm sorry God arranged it that way. She should have been more considerate. But She's done what She's done. Now we have to decide if the cost of the test is worth the benefit. *And your data shows that a benefit is there.*

Mr. Medical Statistician, with some indignation: "No it's not. At conventional levels of significance there is *no effect*."

Deirdre, with more indignation: Nonsense. You are trying, alas, to make a qualitative judgment of existence. Compare the poor, benighted Samuelsonian "theorist." *We always in science need How Much, not Whether.* The effect is empirically there, whatever the noise is. If someone called "Help, help!" in a faint voice, in the midst of lots of noise, so that at the 1% level of significance (the satisfactorily low probability that you will be embarrassed by a false alarm) it could be that she's saying "Kelp, kelp!" (which arose perhaps because she was in a heated argument about a word proposed in a game of Scrabble), *you wouldn't go to her rescue?*

The relevant and quantitative question about routine mammograms, which has recently been reopened, is the balance of cost and benefit, since there could be costs (such as deaths from intrusive tests resulting from false positives) that offset the admittedly slight gain from starting as early as age 40. But suppose, as was long believed, that the costs do not offset the gain. That the net gain is slight is no comfort to the (few) people who die unnecessarily at 42 or 49 on account of Mr. Medical Statistician's gross misunderstanding of the proper role of statistics in scientific inquiries. A death is a death. The over-50 people are killing patients. Maybe only slightly more than zero patients. But more than zero is murder. [At this insult Mr. Medical Statistician leaps up and storms out of the room: I told you it was difficult to persuade the insiders; I wish I had a softer rhetoric to offer which would bring amoral idiots like Mr. Medical Statistician and Mr. Econometrician around gently; but as you can see it's just not in me.]

Or consider the aspirin-and-heart-attack studies. Researchers were testing the effects of administering half an aspirin a day to men who had already suffered a heart attack. To do the experiment correctly they gave one group the aspirin and the other a placebo. But they soon discovered—well short of conventional levels of statistical significance—that the aspirin reduced reoccurrences of heart attacks by about a third. What did they do? Did they go on with the study until they got a large enough sample of dead placebo-getters to be sure of their finding at levels of statistical significance that would make the referees of cardiology journals happy? Of course not: that would have been shockingly (though not unprecedently) unethical. They stopped the study, and gave everyone aspirin. (A *New Yorker* cartoon around the same time made the point, showing a tombstone inscribed, "John Smith, Member, Placebo Group.")

Or consider public opinion polls about who is going to win the next presidential election. These always come hedged about with warnings that the "margin of error is 2% plus or minus." So is the claim that prediction of a presidential election six months before it happens is only 2% off? Give me a break. What is being reported is the *sampling* error (and only at conventional levels of significance, themselves arbitrary). An error caused, say, by the revelation two months down the road that one of the candidates is an active child molester is not reckoned as part of "the error." You can see that a shell game is being performed here. The statement of a "probable error" of 2% is silly. A tiny part of all the errors that can afflict a prediction of a far-off political event is being elevated to the rhetorical status of *The* Error. "My under streetlight sampling theory is very bright, so let's search for the keys under the streetlight, even though I lost them in the dark." Get serious.

The point here is that such silliness utterly dominates empirical economics. In a study of all the empirical articles in the *American Economic Review* in the 1980s it was discovered that fully 96% of them confused statistical and substantive significance (look at *The Rhetoric of Economics*, 2nd ed.; or at Stephen Ziliak and Deirdre McCloskey, "The Standard Error of Regression,"

Journal of Economic Literature, March 1996; check it out on JSTOR; we are writing a paper examining the same journal in the 1990s; bad news: the sin has gotten more prevalent, not less).

The problem is that a number fitted from the world's experiments can be important economically without being noise-free. And it can be wonderfully noise-free without being important.

On the one hand: It's completely obvious, you will agree, that a "statistically insignificant" number can be very significant for some human purpose. If you really, truly want to know how the North American Free Trade Agreement affected the average worker in the United States, then it's too bad if the data are noisy, *but that's not the point*. You really, truly want to know it. You have to go with what God has provided.

And on the other hand: It is also completely obvious that a "statistically significant" result can be *in*significant for any human purpose. When you are trying to explain the rise and fall of the stock market it may be that the fit (so-called: it means how closely the data line up) is very "tight" for some crazy variable, say skirt lengths (for a long while the correlation was actually quite good). *But it doesn't matter*: the variable is obviously crazy. Who cares how closely it fits? For a long time in Britain the number of ham radio operator licenses granted annually was very highly correlated with the number of people certified insane. Very funny. So?

In short, statistical significance is neither necessary nor sufficient for a result to be scientifically significant. Most of the time it is irrelevant. *A researcher is simply committing a scientific error to use it* as it is used in economics and the other social sciences and in medical science and (a strange one, this) population biology *as an all-purpose way of judging whether a number is large enough to matter*. Mattering is a human matter; the numbers figure, but after collecting them the mattering has to be decided finally by *us*; mattering does not *inhere* in a number.

The point is just common sense. It is not subtle or controversial. But thousands of scientists, and among them almost all modern economists, are utterly confused about it.

Physics and chemistry, though of course highly numerical, hardly ever use statistical significance (check it out for yourself: I have in the journal *Science*, for example). Economists and those others use it compulsively, mechanically, erroneously to provide a non-controversial way of deciding whether or not a number is large. You can't do it this way. No competent statistical theorist has disagreed with me on this point since Neyman and Pearson in 1933. *There is no mechanical procedure that can take over the last, crucial step of an inquiry into the world, asking How Much in human terms that matter.*

My argument is not against statistics in empirical work, no more than it is against mathematics in theoretical work. It is against certain very particular and peculiar practices of economic science and a few other fields. Economics has fallen for qualitative "results" in "theory" and significant/insignificant "results" in "empirical work." You can see the similarity between the two. Both are looking for on/off findings that do not require any tiresome inquiry into How Much, how big is big, what is an important variable, How Much exactly is its oomph. Both are looking for machines to produce publishable articles. In this last they have succeeded since Samuelson spoke out loud and bold beyond the dreams of intellectual avarice. Bad science—using qualitative theorems with no quantitative oomph and statistical significance *also* with no quantitative oomph—has driven out good.

The progress of economic science has been seriously damaged. You can't believe anything that comes out of the Two Sins. Not a word. It is all nonsense, which future generations of economists are going to have to do all over again. Most of what appears in the best journals of economics is unscientific rubbish. I find this unspeakably sad. All my friends, my dear, dear friends in economics, have been wasting their time. You can see why I am agitated about the Two Sins. They are vigorous, difficult, demanding activities, like hard chess problems. But they are worthless as science.

The physicist Richard Feynman called such activities Cargo Cult Science. Certain New Guinea tribesmen had prospered mightily during the Second World War when the American military disgorged its cargo to fight the Japanese. After the War the tribesmen wanted the prosperity to come back. So they started a "cargo cult." Out of local materials they built mock airports and mock transport planes. They did an amazingly good job: the cargo-cult airports really do look like airports, the planes like planes. The only trouble is, they aren't actually. Feynman called sciences he didn't like "cargo cult sciences" (he was, ill-advisedly I think, going after sociology: apparently he was not acquainted with the considerable amount of good, non-statistical-significance yet quantitative and empirical and theoretically meaningful sociology, such as long ago that of C. Wright Mills). By "cargo cult" he meant that they looked like science, had all that hard math and statistics, plenty of long words; but actual science, actual inquiry into the world, was not going on.

I am afraid that my science of economics has come to the same point. Paul Samuelson, though a splendid man and a wonderful economist (honestly), is a symbol of the pointlessness of qualitative theorems. Samuelson, actually, is more than merely a symbol—he made and taught and defended the Two Sins, at one time almost single-handedly. It was a brave stance. But it had terrible outcomes. Samuelson advocated the "scientific" program of producing *qualitative* theorems, developing qualitative-theorem-generating-functions (I am making an insider's statistical joke: ha, ha; such is economic humor), such as "revealed preference" and "overlapping generations" models and above all the machinery of Max U. He was involved also (it turns out somewhat surprisingly) in the early propagation of significance testing, the "scientific" method of empirical work running on statistical significance [technical remark: *sans* loss functions], through his first Ph.D. student, Lawrence Klein (Nobel 1980). Two sins, one scientist.

So it is only fair to call both the sins of modern economics Samuelsonian. It is rather similar to the situation in linguistics: *their* Great MIT Leader is Noam Chomsky. Chomsky's mechanical approach to grammar, fiercely denying pragmatics and therefore the main finding of the humanities in the twentieth century, blocks progress. So too economics. Until economics stops believing, contrary to its own principles, that an intellectual free lunch is to be gotten from qualitative theorems and statistical significance it will be stuck on the ground waiting at the cargo-cult airport, at any rate in its high-end activities uninterested in (Really) How Much. High-end theoretical and econometric papers will be published. Careers will be made, thank you very much. Many outstanding fellows (and no women) will get chairs at Princeton and Chicago. But our understanding of the economic world will continue to be crippled by the spreading, ramifying, hideous sins.

Woe, woe is me. *Oy vey ist mir.* Pity the poor economists. The sins of economics come from pride in formalization, the making of great machines and monsters:

> *...and called me Sin, and for a sign*
> *Portentous held me; but familiar grown,*

*I pleased, and with attractive graces won
The most averse.*

And pity, I repeat, poor old Deirdre, who appears to be doomed to keep making these arguments, showing more and more plainly that the two main methods of academic economics are nonsense, without being believed.

Cassandra, you know, was the most beautiful of the daughters of Priam, King of Troy. The god Apollo fell for her and made her a prophetess. In exchange he wanted sexual favors, which she refused. So he cursed her, in a most malicious way. He had already given her the power of prophecy, to know for example what would happen to a science that refused to ask seriously How Much. His curse was to add that though she would continue to be correct in her prophecies, *no one would believe her*.

> *Cassandra [to Trojan economists proposing to bring the wooden horse into the city]*: The horse is filled with enemy soldiers! If you bring it into the city, economics is lost! *Please* don't!
> *Leading Trojan Economist*: Uh, yeah, I see what you mean, Cassie. Good point. Enemy soldiers. Inside. City lost. Qualitative theorems useless for a science. Statistical significance without a loss function equally useless. Economics ruined. Thanks *very* much for your prophecy. *Great* contribution. Love your stuff. *[Turning to colleagues]* Okay, guys, let's bring that sucker in!